The Four Level SPELLING TIME

Master 150 Spelling Words Through Art & Logic!

Poems By: Charity J. Thayer & Mimi Thayer
Produced By: Sarah Janisse Brown
Artwork By: Tolik Trishkin
Cover By: Sarah Brown
Published By: \The Thinking Tree Publishing
Company LLC Copyright 2016

150 Do-It-Yourself Spelling Words

Above	December	June	Smell
Again	Degrees	Leaves	Smile
Along	Delicious	Listen	Snow
Always	Falling	Looks	Snowballs
April	Favorite	Love	Snowing
Arrives	Feathers	Love	Snowman
August	February	Lunch	Someone
Autumn	Floating	Magic	Something
Bake	Flowers	Make	Special
Beach	Fly	May	Spend
Beauty	Flying	Might	Splash
Begin	Foxes	Minute	Spring
Berries	Freeze	Necklace	Still
Best	Friendly	Never	Summer
Bird	Friends	Nothing	Sunny
Bloom	Friendship	November	Swim
Brand	Frosty	Nuts	Taste
Breeze	Fur	October	Tell
Bright	Gather	Orange	That's
Bring	Glow	Out	Together
Brings	Glowing	Outdoors	Trail
Build	Grounds	Over	Treasure
Bundle	Growing	Peach	Tree Air
Bunny	Hands	Picnic	Truly
Butterfly	Happy	Prance	Umbrella
Cake	Hear	Puddles	Under
Calling	He'll	Quite	Warm
Carries	Holding	Race	Watch
Castles	Hours	Remember	Water
Chirping	Hours	Sailboat	Weather
Climb	How	Seagulls	Welcome
Cocoa	Ice	Season	We'll
Come	Into	September	Which
Cookies	I'll	Shell	Will
Cozy	January	Skate	Winter
Crab	July	Sky	World
Dance	Jumping		You'll

TABLE OF CONTENTS:

5...... Spelling Poems, Art & Logic Games

52..... Fun-Spelling Practice Pages

80..... What Words Can You Spell?

95..... Creative Writing Prompts

112.... Draw Each Season

114.... Make Your Own Calendar

PARENT & TEACHER INSTRUCTIONS:

If your child can not read well, read the spelling poem to the child three times. Ask your child to repeat after each line the third time you read it together.

If your child can read all you need to do is provide the child with colored pencils, gel pens and fun music to work to! The child should complete two pages each day.

SPELLING POEMS ART & LOGIC GAMES

ONE DAY IN MAY

One day in MAY I will play
With a BUNNY on a SUNNY day.

We'll SPEND the HOURS
Picking FLOWERS.

I'll SMILE at a BUTTERFLY
And WATCH a ladybug PRANCE by.

My FRIENDS and I will SMILE and sing
About the BEAUTY and MAGIC of SPRING!

Color the SPELLING Words.

Use Gel Pens, Crayons, or Colored Pencils to Complete This Illustration.

ONE DAY IN MAY

One day in ___ I will play
With a _____ on a _____ day.

We'll _____ the _____
Picking _____.

I'll _____ at a _____
And _____ a ladybug _____ by.

My _____ and I will _____ and sing
About the _____ and _____ of _____!

Write the Missing SPELLING Words.

What is Missing? Use a Black Gel Pen to Draw the Missing Parts.

THE JOY OF JUNE

In JUNE YOU'LL see me FLYING by.
I'LL find a FRIENDLY bird to ride.

WE'LL stop to SMELL spring flowers.
Every MINUTE will feel like HOURS.

HE'LL fly with me INTO the sky,
And we will be BEST FRIENDS for life!

It WILL be so fun to see,
What the WORLD LOOKS like from a tree!

Use Gel Pens, Crayons, or Colored Pencils to Complete This Illustration.

THE JOY OF JUNE

In____ ___-__ see me_____ by.
_-__ find a _____ bird to ride.

__-__stop to _____ spring flowers.
Every _____ will feel like _____.

__-__fly with me ____ the sky
And we will be ____ _____ for life!

It ____ be so fun to see,
What the _____ _____ like from a tree!

12

What is Missing? Use a Black Gel Pen to Draw the Missing Parts.

JULY AT THE BEACH

JULY MIGHT be my FAVORITE month,
To BUILD sand CASTLES in the SUMMER sun!

I'll go with all my FRIENDS to the BEACH,
And in my LUNCH I'll pack a PEACH.

While the SEAGULLS soar up ABOVE
I'll make a shell NECKLACE for SOMEONE I love!

Then we'll all SWIM, SPLASH, and play
Yes, THAT'S what we'll do on a hot JULY day!

Use Gel Pens, Crayons, or Colored Pencils to Complete This Illustration.

Use Gel Pens, Crayons, or Colored Pencils to Complete This Illustration.

JULY AT THAT BEACH

____ _____ be my _____ month,
To _____ sand _____ in the _____ sun!

I'll go with all my _____ to the _____,
And in my _____ I'll pack a _____.

While the _____ fly up _____,
I'll make a shell _____ for _____ I love!

Then we'll all ____, _____ and play
Yes, _____ what we'll do on a hot ____day!

Use Gel Pens, Crayons, or Colored Pencils to Complete This Illustration.

ALL ABOUT AUGUST

In AUGUST the days are SUNNY and hot,
WHICH is SOMETHING that I like a lot!

And NOTHING makes me QUITE as glad,
As FLOATING ALONG on a lily pad.

The air is WARM but the WATER is cool,
So I'll MAKE a big SPLASH in my pool!

Oh HOW I do LOVE to go OUT and play,
In the SUMMER sun on an AUGUST day!

Use Gel Pens, Crayons, or Colored Pencils to Complete This Illustration.

ALL ABOUT AUGUST

In _____ the days are _____ and hot,
_____ is _____ that I like a lot!

And _____ makes me _____ as glad,
As _____ _____ on a lily pad.

The air is ____ but the _____ is cool,
So I'll ____ a big _____ in my pool!

Oh ___ I do ____ to go ___ and play,
In the _____ sun on an _____ day!

What is Missing? Use a Black Gel Pen to Draw the Missing Parts.

What is Missing? Use a Black Gel Pen to Draw the Missing Parts.

SWEET SEPTEMBER

In SEPTEMBER I will REMEMBER
That AUTUMN with friends is ALWAYS better

We'll have a PICNIC UNDER a tree.
The FOXES WILL BRING good things to eat!

HOLDING HANDS WE'LL DANCE around,
While AUTUMN LEAVES fall to the GROUND!

What is Missing? Use a Black Gel Pen to Draw the Missing Parts.

SWEET SEPTEMBER

In _____ I will _____
That _____ with friends is _____ better

We'll have a _____ _____ a tree.
The _____ ____ _____ good things to eat!

_____ _____ _____ _____ around,
While _____ _____ fall to the _____!

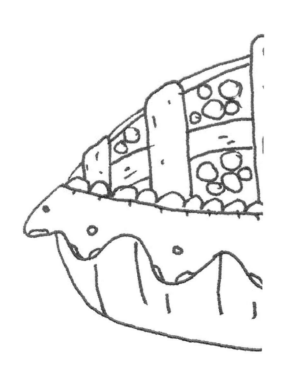

Use Gel Pens, Crayons, or Colored Pencils to Complete This Illustration.

OH OCTOBER!

Now it's OCTOBER and friends COME OVER!
First we CLIMB big trees TOGETHER!

Then play in the BRIGHT ORANGE LEAVES.
Next we'll GATHER NUTS and seeds!

Getting ready for the WINTER WEATHER,
Is fun with friends with FUR OR FEATHERS!

My friend the bunny happily CARRIES,
His basket to fill with NUTS AND BERRIES!

What is Missing? Use a Black Gel Pen to Draw the Missing Parts.

OH OCTOBER!

Now it's _____ and friends ____ ____!
 First we _____ big trees _____!

Then play in the _____ _____ _____.
 Next we'll _____ ____ and seeds!

 Getting ready for the _____ _____,
Is fun with friends with ___ __ _____!

 My friend the bunny happily _____,
His basket to fill with ____ ___ _____!

Use Gel Pens, Crayons, or Colored Pencils to Complete This Illustration.

NOVEMBER RAIN

In **November** it might rain and pour!
But we will still go play **outdoors**!

I'll **bring my umbrella** and rain boots too!
So I can **splash in puddles** with you!

I don't mind if it's rain or shine,
A **friend like you** is great all of the time!

We'll **sing and dance** as the winds blow!
Until December **brings the snow**!

Use Gel Pens, Crayons, or Colored Pencils to Complete This Illustration.

NOVEMBER RAIN

In NOVEMBER it might rain and pour!
But we will still go play OUTDOORS!

I'll BRING MY UMBRELLA and rain boots too!
So I can SPLASH IN PUDDLES with you!

I don't mind if it's rain or shine,
A FRIEND LIKE YOU is great all of the time!

We'll SING AND DANCE as the winds blow!
Until December BRINGS THE SNOW!

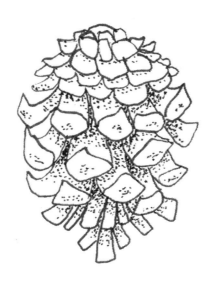

Use Gel Pens, Crayons, or Colored Pencils to Complete This Illustration.

DECEMBER DAYS

When **December** comes we'll **gather together!**
No matter how **cold or frosty** the weather!

By a fire so **cozy and bright**
We'll drink **hot cocoa** by firelight.

Outside there may be **ice and snow**
But we'll be warm by the **fire's glow.**

It will be a **special day** to remember
that a **friendship** like ours is **truly a treasure!**

Use Gel Pens, Crayons, or Colored Pencils to Complete This Illustration.

DECEMBER DAYS

When _____ comes we'll _____ _____!
No matter how ____ __ _____ the weather!

By a fire so ____ ___ _____
We'll drink ___ _____ by firelight.

_____ there may be ___ ___ ____
But we'll be warm by the _____ ____.

It will be a _____ ___ to remember
that a _____ like ours is _____ a _____!

Use Gel Pens, Crayons, or Colored Pencils to Complete This Illustration.

JANUARY SNOW

In <u>January</u> I will play,
With bear and bunny <u>every</u> day!

I will <u>bundle</u> up in a warm coat and hat
We'll build a <u>snowman</u>, <u>imagine</u> that!

<u>Snowflakes</u> will be <u>falling</u> all the while,
And our snowman will have a <u>happy</u> smile!

Then I'll make <u>snowballs</u> that we can throw!
Oh how I <u>love</u> to play in the <u>snow</u>!

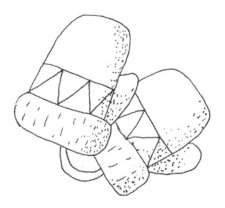

Use Gel Pens, Crayons, or Colored Pencils to Complete This Illustration.

JANUARY SNOW

In _____ play
With _____ day!

I will _____ and hat
We'll _____ that!

Snowflakes _____ while,
And our _____ smile!

Then _____ throw!
Oh _____ snow!

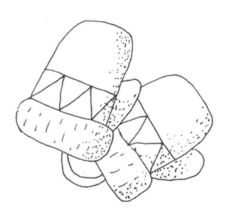

Use Gel Pens, Crayons, or Colored Pencils to Complete This Illustration.

FEBRUARY FUN

In FEBRUARY snow is STILL falling,
But I can HEAR my good friends CALLING!

"Come OUTSIDE with us to play!
Bring your sled it's SNOWING TODAY!"

We will RACE DOWN the hills of snow,
And CLIMB back to the top!

AGAIN, AGAIN, AGAIN we'll go,
As if we'll NEVER stop!

Use Gel Pens, Crayons, or Colored Pencils to Complete This Illustration.

FEBRUARY FUN

In _____ snow is _____ falling,
But I can ____ my good friends _____!

"Come _____ with us to play!
Bring your sled it's _____ _____!"

We will ____ ____ the hills of snow,
And _____ back to the top!

_____, _____, _____ we'll go,
As if we'll _____ stop!

Use Gel Pens, Crayons, or Colored Pencils to Complete This Illustration.

MARCH MAGIC

In March the flowers BEGIN TO BLOOM.
There will be WARM WEATHER soon!

LISTEN to the birds as they sing,
A happy song to WELCOME SPRING.

I can see the MELTING SNOW!
I can see new FLOWERS GROW!

Oh how I love to SING ALONG
With the birds CHIRPING a springtime song!

Use Gel Pens, Crayons, or Colored Pencils to Complete This Illustration.

MARCH MAGIC

In _____
  There _____!

_____,
  A happy song to _____ _____.

I can _____!
I can _____!

Oh _____
With _____ song!

Use Gel Pens, Crayons, or Colored Pencils to Complete This Illustration.

AMAZING APRIL

As APRIL ARRIVES,
The flowers are GROWING!

The birds are SINGING!
The sun is GLOWING!

There are LEAVES on the trees,
And a lovely spring BREEZE!

I'll GATHER FLOWERS with fox and SNAIL.
Then we'll set off down a BRAND new TRAIL!

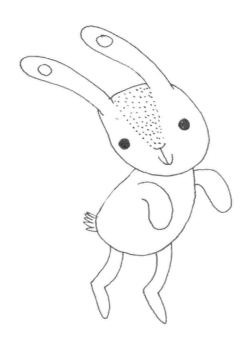

Use Gel Pens, Crayons, or Colored Pencils to Complete This Illustration.

AMAZING APRIL

As _____ _____,
The flowers are _____!

The birds are _____!
The sun is _____!

There are _____ on the trees,
And a lovely spring _____!

I'll _____ _____ with fox and _____.
Then we'll set off down a _____ new _____!

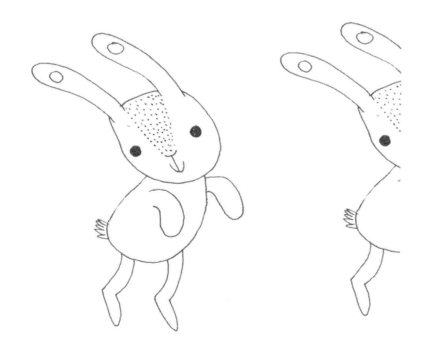

The Four Seasons

FUN-SPELLING PRACTICE PAGES

SPRING
SUMMER
AUTUMN
WINTER

Some fun words to
SPELL IN SPRING!

SPRING

FLOWER

FLY

SKY

MAGIC

BIRD

TUNE

SING

TREE

LEAF

AIR

WINGS

SPRING!

SPRING

It's spring and there is **magic** in the air!
Flowers are **blooming everywhere.**
I **pretend** that I have wings to **soar** up high,
Like a **smiling butterfly**!

I'll help a **butterfly** tend **flowers**,
With my **amazing** flying **powers**!
A **dragonfly** will join the fun
We'll all fly **together** in the springtime sun!

Just **imagine** a girl **flying** high in the trees,
Up there in the pretty, **bright** green **leaves**.
You never **know** what could **happen** in the sky.
Maybe I'll meet a **hummingbird** flying by!

We could **become** good **friends** so true,
And soar **together** in a sky of blue!
We could do so many **lovely** things.
Oh how I **love** the **magic** of **spring**!

SPRING

It's spring and there is _____ in the air!
Flowers are _____ _____.
I _____ that I have wings to ____ up high,
Like a _____ _____!

I'll help a _____ tend _____,
With my _____ flying _____!
A _____ will join the fun
We'll all fly _____ in the springtime sun!

Just _____ a girl _____ high in the trees,
Up there in the pretty, _____ green _____.
You never ____ what could _____ in the sky.
Maybe I'll meet a _____ flying by!

We could _____ good _____ so true,
And soar _____ in a sky of blue!
We could do so many _____ things.
Oh how I ____ the _____ of _____!

Some fun words to SPELL IN SUMMER!

SUMMER

SHELL

TELL

SAILBOAT

JUMPING

SUN

HOT

CRAB

BEACH

WATER

SAND

SUMMER!

SUMMER

It's **summer** and the **weather** is getting hotter.
I'll play with friends down by the **water**.
We can all go to the beach **together**.
I think we'll all be friends **forever**!

Maybe I will find a shell on the **ground**.
Hold it up to my ear and hear the **sound**.
Of waves **crashing** on a **summer** day!
Oh what a **happy** place to play!

Summer sun is **shining** in the sky.
I **think** I'll go for a **sailboat** ride!
My **animal friends** will come along with me.
And we'll sail **together** on the **bright blue** sea.

I'll **bring** my trusty **telescope**.
We'll see some **lovely sights** I hope!
Perhaps some **mountains** that touch the sky,
Or a **smiling** fish **jumping** high!

SUMMER

It's _____ and the _____ is getting hotter.
I'll play with friends down by the _____.
We can all go to the beach _____.
I think we'll all be friends _____!

Maybe I will find a shell on the _____.
Hold it up to my ear and hear the _____.
Of waves _____ on a _____ day!
Oh what a _____ place to play!

Summer sun is _____ in the sky.
I _____ I'll go for a _____ ride!
My _____ _____ will come along with me.
And we'll sail _____ on the _____ ____ sea.

I'll _____ my trusty _____.
We'll see some _____ _____ I hope!
Perhaps some _____ that touch the sky,
Or a _____ fish _____ high!

Some fun words to SPELL IN AUTUMN!

AUTUMN

FALL

LEAVES

TREES

FRIEND

PREPARE

FOOD

ORANGE

BREEZE

ACORNS

YELLOW

Autumn!

AUTUMN

One of the **seasons** I like most of all,
Is **autumn though** some call it fall!
There are **orange**, red, and **yellow leaves**,
Blown by the **breeze** and falling from trees.

I love it when my friends come **around**,
And we pile **leaves** up on the **ground**.
Then we all jump up, up, up and **down**,
While the fall leaves make a **crackling sound**!

Something else we do in fall
Is **prepare** for winter one and all!
My **animal** friends are gathering food,
This is **something** I can help them do!

If I find **acorns**, **squirrel** will be pleased!
He'll run and **store** them in the trees!
How I love to help my **animal** friends!
Now we'll be **ready** when the snow **begins**!

AUTUMN

One of the _____ I like most of all,
Is _____ _____ some call it fall!
There are _____, red, and _____ _____,
_____ by the _____ and falling from trees.

I love it when my friends come _____,
And we pile _____ up on the _____.
Then we all jump up, up, up and ____,
While the fall leaves make a _____ _____!

_____ else we do in fall
Is _____ for winter one and all!
My _____ friends are gathering food,
This is _____ I can help them do!

If I find _____, _____ will be pleased!
He'll run and _____ them in the trees!
How I love to help my _____ friends!
Now we'll be _____ when the snow _____!

Some fun words to
SPELL IN WINTER!

WINTER

DEGREES

SNOW

FREEZE

SKATE

ICE

FRIEND

BAKE

CAKE

SEASON

COOKIES

Winter!

WINTER

Now it is **winter** and there are many **reasons**,
To **enjoy** the coldest of all the **seasons**!
Snow **comes** and things begin to **freeze**,
It might be less than two **degrees**!

But I still think the **weather** is great
To go **outdoors**, if you like to ice skate!
My friend the bear **always** comes calling,
To **skate** with me when the snow is **falling**!

In **winter** you could stay **inside**,
All warm and cozy with **friends** by your **side**!
This is the very best **season** to bake
Cookies, **muffins**, pies and cake!

Imagine all the **lovely treats**
That smell **delicious** and **taste** so **sweet**!
Oh we will have a lovely **time**,
Its cold **outdoors** but it's here warm **inside**!

WINTER

Now it is _____ and there are many _____,
 To _____ the coldest of all the _____!
Snow _____ and things begin to _____,
 It might be less than two _____!

 But I still think the _____ is great
To go _____, if you like to ice skate!
 My friend the bear _____ comes calling,
To _____ with me when the snow is _____!

 In _____ you could stay _____,
All warm and cozy with _____ by your side!
 This is the very best _____ to bake
 _____, _____, pies and cake!

 _____ all the _____ _____
That smell _____ and _____ so _____!
 Oh we will have a lovely ____,
Its cold _____ but it's here warm _____!

What Words You Can Spell? Circle Them!

Above	December	June	Smell
Again	Degrees	Leaves	Smile
Along	Delicious	Listen	Snow
Always	Falling	Looks	Snowballs
April	Favorite	Love	Snowing
Arrives	Feathers	Love	Snowman
August	February	Lunch	Someone
Autumn	Floating	Magic	Something
Bake	Flowers	Make	Special
Beach	Fly	May	Spend
Beauty	Flying	Might	Splash
Begin	Foxes	Minute	Spring
Berries	Freeze	Necklace	Still
Best	Friendly	Never	Summer
Bird	Friends	Nothing	Sunny
Bloom	Friendship	November	Swim
Brand	Frosty	Nuts	Taste
Breeze	Fur	October	Tell
Bright	Gather	Orange	That's
Bring	Glow	Out	Together
Brings	Glowing	Outdoors	Trail
Build	Grounds	Over	Treasure
Bundle	Growing	Peach	Tree Air
Bunny	Hands	Picnic	Truly
Butterfly	Happy	Prance	Umbrella
Cake	Hear	Puddles	Under
Calling	He'll	Quite	Warm
Carries	Holding	Race	Watch
Castles	Hours	Remember	Water
Chirping	Hours	Sailboat	Weather
Climb	How	Seagulls	Welcome
Cocoa	Ice	Season	We'll
Come	Into	September	Which
Cookies	I'll	Shell	Will
Cozy	January	Skate	Winter
Crab	July	Sky	World
Dance	Jumping		You'll

What Spelling Words Do You Need to Practice?

Write a Story With Your Practice Words:

What Spelling Words Do You Need to Practice?

Write a Story With Your Practice Words:

What Spelling Words Do You Need to Practice?

Write a Story With Your Practice Words:

What Spelling Words Do You Need to Practice?

Write a Story With Your Practice Words:

What Spelling Words Do You Need to Practice?

Write a Story With Your Practice Words:

Circle All the Words You Can Spell:

Above	December	June	Smell
Again	Degrees	Leaves	Smile
Along	Delicious	Listen	Snow
Always	Falling	Looks	Snowballs
April	Favorite	Love	Snowing
Arrives	Feathers	Love	Snowman
August	February	Lunch	Someone
Autumn	Floating	Magic	Something
Bake	Flowers	Make	Special
Beach	Fly	May	Spend
Beauty	Flying	Might	Splash
Begin	Foxes	Minute	Spring
Berries	Freeze	Necklace	Still
Best	Friendly	Never	Summer
Bird	Friends	Nothing	Sunny
Bloom	Friendship	November	Swim
Brand	Frosty	Nuts	Taste
Breeze	Fur	October	Tell
Bright	Gather	Orange	That's
Bring	Glow	Out	Together
Brings	Glowing	Outdoors	Trail
Build	Grounds	Over	Treasure
Bundle	Growing	Peach	Tree Air
Bunny	Hands	Picnic	Truly
Butterfly	Happy	Prance	Umbrella
Cake	Hear	Puddles	Under
Calling	He'll	Quite	Warm
Carries	Holding	Race	Watch
Castles	Hours	Remember	Water
Chirping	Hours	Sailboat	Weather
Climb	How	Seagulls	Welcome
Cocoa	Ice	Season	We'll
Come	Into	September	Which
Cookies	I'll	Shell	Will
Cozy	January	Skate	Winter
Crab	July	Sky	World
Dance	Jumping		You'll

The Four Seasons

CREATIVE WRITING PROMPTS

SPRING
SUMMER
AUTUMN
WINTER

SPRING!

March, April, May & June!
Make a List of 15 FUN Things to do in Spring:

Use These Spelling Words to Tell a Story!

SPRING
FLOWER
FLY
SKY
MAGIC
BIRD
TUNE
SING
TREE
LEAF
AIR
WINGS

Draw a picture here to go with your story:

It was a warm day in early spring the snow was melting and the sun was shining! You put on your rain boots and borrowed a big bucket.

SUMMER!

June, July, August & September!
Make a List of 15 FUN Things to do in Summer:

Use These Spelling Words to Tell a Story!

- SUMMER
- SHELL
- TELL
- SAILBOAT
- JUMPING
- SUN
- HOT
- CRAB
- BEACH
- WATER
- SAND

Draw a picture here to go with your story:

Summer is coming and our family is planning a vacation! My mom asked me where I would like to go! She said that I could bring two of my best friends!

Autumn!

September, October, November & December!
Make a List of 15 FUN Things to do in Autumn:

Use These Spelling Words to Tell a Story!

- AUTUMN
- FALL
- LEAVES
- TREES
- FRIEND
- PREPARE
- FOOD
- ORANGE
- BREEZE
- ACORNS
- YELLOW

Draw a picture here to go with your story:

It is autumn and the leaves are falling. Your friends are trying to decide what to do on Saturday after everyone finishes chores. You are thinking about ways to earn money, your friends are thinking about baking muffins!

Winter!

December, January, February & March!
Make a List of 15 FUN Things to do in Winter:

Use These Spelling Words to Tell a Story!

WINTER
DEGREES
SNOW
FREEZE
SKATE
ICE
FRIEND
BAKE
CAKE
COOKIES
SEASON

Draw a picture here to go with your story:

One morning you looked out the window. The whole world was white! There were only animal tracks in the freshly fallen snow.

Draw a Picture of SPRING:

Draw a Picture of SUMMER:

Draw a Picture of AUTUMN:

Draw a Picture of WINTER:

Make Your Own Calendar

Sunday	Monday	Tuesday	Wednesday	Thursday	Friday	Saturday

Sunday	Monday	Tuesday	Wednesday	Thursday	Friday	Saturday

Sunday	Monday	Tuesday	Wednesday	Thursday	Friday	Saturday

Sunday	Monday	Tuesday	Wednesday	Thursday	Friday	Saturday

Sunday	Monday	Tuesday	Wednesday	Thursday	Friday	Saturday

Sunday	Monday	Tuesday	Wednesday	Thursday	Friday	Saturday

Sunday	Monday	Tuesday	Wednesday	Thursday	Friday	Saturday

Sunday	Monday	Tuesday	Wednesday	Thursday	Friday	Saturday

Sunday	Monday	Tuesday	Wednesday	Thursday	Friday	Saturday

Sunday	Monday	Tuesday	Wednesday	Thursday	Friday	Saturday

Sunday	Monday	Tuesday	Wednesday	Thursday	Friday	Saturday

Sunday	Monday	Tuesday	Wednesday	Thursday	Friday	Saturday

Sunday	Monday	Tuesday	Wednesday	Thursday	Friday	Saturday

Sunday	Monday	Tuesday	Wednesday	Thursday	Friday	Saturday

Sunday	Monday	Tuesday	Wednesday	Thursday	Friday	Saturday

Sunday	Monday	Tuesday	Wednesday	Thursday	Friday	Saturday

Sunday	Monday	Tuesday	Wednesday	Thursday	Friday	Saturday

Sunday	Monday	Tuesday	Wednesday	Thursday	Friday	Saturday

Sunday	Monday	Tuesday	Wednesday	Thursday	Friday	Saturday

Sunday	Monday	Tuesday	Wednesday	Thursday	Friday	Saturday

Sunday	Monday	Tuesday	Wednesday	Thursday	Friday	Saturday

Sunday	Monday	Tuesday	Wednesday	Thursday	Friday	Saturday

Made in the USA
Columbia, SC
13 December 2024

48030516R00078